THE CLEARING

THE CLEARING

POEMS BY ALLISON ADAIR

Max Ritvo Prize For Poetry | Selected by Henri Cole

MILKWEED EDITIONS

Published 2020 by Milkweed Editions
Printed in Canada
Cover design by Mary Austin Speaker
Cover art by Hagar Vardimon
Author photo by Max Green
20 21 22 23 24   5 4 3 2 1
First Edition

Milkweed Editions, an independent nonprofit publisher, gratefully acknowledges sustaining
support from the Alan B. Slifka Foundation and its president, Riva Ariella Ritvo-Slifka; the
Ballard Spahr Foundation; *Copper Nickel*; the McKnight Foundation; the National Endowment
for the Arts; the National Poetry Series; the Target Foundation; and other generous contributions
from foundations, corporations, and individuals. Also, this activity is made possible by the voters of
Minnesota through a Minnesota State Arts Board Operating Support grant, thanks to a legislative
appropriation from the arts and cultural heritage fund. For a full listing of Milkweed Editions
supporters, please visit milkweed.org.

Library of Congress Cataloging-in-Publication Data
   Names: Adair, Allison, author.
   Title: The clearing : poems / Allison Adair.
   Description: First edition. | Minneapolis, Minnesota : Milkweed Editions,
      2020. | Summary: "The Clearing is the debut collection of poems from the
      winner of the 2019 Max Ritvo Poetry Prize, Allison Adair"-- Provided by
      publisher.
   Identifiers: LCCN 2019054069 (print) | LCCN 2019054070 (ebook) | ISBN
      9781571315144 (hardcover ; acid-free paper) | ISBN 9781571317407 (ebook)

   Subjects: LCGFT: Poetry.
   Classification: LCC PS3601.D347 C57 2020 (print) | LCC PS3601.D347
      (ebook) | DDC 811/.6--dc23
   LC record available at https://lccn.loc.gov/2019054069
   LC ebook record available at https://lccn.loc.gov/2019054070

Milkweed Editions is committed to ecological stewardship. We strive to align our book produc-
tion practices with this principle, and to reduce the impact of our operations in the environment.
We are a member of the Green Press Initiative, a nonprofit coalition of publishers, manufacturers,
and authors working to protect the world's endangered forests and conserve natural resources. *The
Clearing* was printed on acid-free 100% postconsumer-waste paper by Friesens Corporation.

For my parents

For my sister

CONTENTS

THE CLEARING

THE CLEARING

What if this time instead of crumbs the girl drops
teeth, her own, what else does she have, and the prince

or woodcutter or brother or man musty with beard and
thick in the pants collects the teeth with a wide rustic hand,

holds their gray roots to a nostril to smell the fresh
feminine rot, fingers the bony stems of her

fear, born of watered-down broths, of motherlessness,
of an owl's sharp beak crooking back around into itself?

The wolf licks his parts with a sandpaper tongue
and just like that we've got ourselves a familiar victim.

It is written: the world's fluids shall rush into a single birch
tree and there's the girl, lying in a clearing we've never seen

but know is ours. Undergrowth rattles like the shank
of a loose pen. We'll write this story again and again,

how her mouth blooms to its raw venous throat—that tunnel
of marbled wetness, beefy, muted, new, pillow for our star

sapphire, our sluggish prospecting—and how dark birds come
after, to dress the wounds, no, to peck her sockets clean.

I

AFTER THE POLICE HAVE BEEN CALLED

I'm not sure what I imagined, but I thought
the lapis sash of a mallard's wing meant joy

was everyone's destiny. That it was tucked in
if only you knew how to look, how to route salt

to the sides of your tongue, bitter to the back.
I preened in the gloss of black ice. Our vows

lassoed the night sky—tried to—each word a flint-
dipped sparkler, a nest of lightning or a thrashing

fuse. Wasn't that love?

                         Not the way violins are
made, maple soaked, warped, planed till sound

bloats wood's ancient fissures. Not like the bow, slow-
combed, pale horsehair secured, capped in wax.

When you begin to hate a man, his stunt fingers
swell with fat. His red face sweats strawberry rot.

Like a stuck pig, the door, if locked, brays and grunts
at his boot-strike, shoulder-strike. The town is small,

but it's his. You dial, wanting someone to marvel
with you, to witness that cheap bolt as it holds.

To fix the cornered nuthatch three-quarters dead, still
resisting in the cat's mouth, still dreaming of flight.

LETTER TO MY NIECE, IN SILVERTON, COLORADO

Someday you will watch your mother lean on the rim of the sink to wash dishes in a way she never has before and you will wonder if she was ever young. I'm here to tell you that cars are so much quieter than they used to be, at a stop sign you never know whose turn it is. It wasn't always like that. It used to be you could hear an engine from down the road, and know whose it was and where it could take somebody. Your mother's hair used to be so light it glowed. On the summer boardwalk people stopped to remark. Men asked questions. It got to where we could hardly make it to the Gravitron before the line snaked back to the sea. Those days there weren't so many metal railings. If your timing was right you could get close to things. To the ride itself, pistons gasping so loud you could almost see the thrust of greased air. To gears joining and unjoining themselves inside a dense black band. To your sister's impatient hand chiming pink shells on a bracelet, new, from someone we didn't know. She never answered them, just looked ahead and grabbed my wrist. *Don't look people in the eye.* It used to be that you got instructions. Then every ride began playing its own music. Your mother's white hair faded against the punched paper reams of old calliope, and soon no one could predict flats or sharps. I'm trying to say that waves used to roll in, then back out. That you could count on the moon to give off a little light. It used to be that idling cars might have stopped for the tide, to watch it slide its wet hands up the day's sand line. But dusk grew tired of resisting, I guess. Or maybe the cars had always been waiting for us, waiting patiently for us to come to the window. If we got close enough they knew they could stir the tiny oceans lapping in our shells.

AS FOR THE GLOSSY GREEN TRACTOR YOU WERE

As for the glossy green tractor you were
expecting. The dirt pen, hen looking through
to a white cloud. As for her slack wattles, as if
country had so much time. For every one you
see, a hundred jolting necks. Cow tongue sliced
for a lunch box. Admit it: you're lost. Let the chicken
hawk stop circling, you'll see his red tail's
really a brick. Beak worn from working hard
bones. The hurt of it. Wet rot that worms in
from west of west of town, then moves on.

The well cap's been missing—kids still play
rocket, spike, disappear. Anything you hear
like dough lifted or slammed on a stone
is neither. Don't come close. Don't wipe
your forehead with a sleeve. Uncooked
field corn bursts for any mouth—that's design.
And the road that brought you here lies too
close to the speedway for stars. Bar's closed.
Young and younger fumble at each other by
a swollen creek. Under them, larvae drill snails.

The world's getting bigger—truth is hard
to see. Try shaking a firefly until he vomits
daylight. (Here's wisdom they don't print.)
The neon gel smeared across your hand can light
the way. Go ahead. Reach out for something dark.

MISCARRIAGE

The colors are off. Muted, like a confession.
That's what drew me to it, this rug
in the middle of my living
room floor. I found it enchanting.

We'd lost our first
to moths—what could we do?
It was their season.
I didn't know how to save things.

This one would be different.
Woven into the pattern were women
facing one another, each passing
a small, blurry object to the next. I was

determined to take better care this time—
swept and scrubbed, tried
to comb out of the fibers anything wrong, unnatural.
The wood planks bowed as I worked.

But something had already laid its eggs
in a place I couldn't reach.
The women in the carpet looked away
as if they knew what they'd come to deliver.

WEEK SIX OF THE FIRE

after Aimee Nezhukumatathil

I have faith in the spindle of an aspen.
I have faith in its sugar-drenched bark, in the scorched-butterfly
bruise left by an elk's incisors. I have faith in the tree's skeleton
branch, in the flat stems helping each leaf survive the whiplash of mountain wind, I have
faith in anything with a steady tremble. In light that leaks through.

I, too, once trusted the itch of a velvet antler
to carry my hunger toward a grove. I trusted
something—instinct, desire, the buck's lung-shaped tracks—to keep me moving
through the fire, through scarves of molten citrine wafting in a vaulted sky, which is to say
out from under your body, beyond the memory of its long, easy weight,
its stack of ashen bones.

The fire blooms into its sixth week.

My faith grows heavy, a cloud baggy with grim rain.

SELF-PORTRAIT AS CENOTAPH

Gettysburg, 1986

Then without further violence green shoots break through and the men
arrive as usual with their metal detectors. They've come for bullets, war
coins, a button from the chest of either army. We hear their boots pause

on the step and wait for a thick ambitious finger to darken the unfamiliar
bell. The hyacinth swells. A patinaed eagle means more than a good day
of digging and my mother says yes quickly, hand on the knob.

In its gummy web, our spider folds in like a travel brush. Mostly the men come in
the day, to barrow behind alien orbs, crosshatching grass. From my window they look
like showoffs at the shore, walking invisible dogs. They're unzipping

sound to see what's beneath, probing the soft red mouth of our yard. I want to run
out and guard the tulips in their beds, the nests underground that no one can
see: rabbit, vole, yellowjacket. But they haven't come for these, anything living is good

as dead. A man pulls brown from the ground, an ancient weary worm
—no, wrong, rusted bridle bit still bitter in the hinge, rotten gunpowder
lining the jowls of history's sad horse.
$\qquad\qquad\qquad\qquad\qquad$ The man runs a tongue along his teeth,

Later he eases quarters into my young palm, silver somewhere on the scale
between money and memorial. Trim wasps, each someone's tender drummer, spill out
of the cracked shale hive, spooked by their own droning, then flatten to enter

the house's gap, that space between flimsy white siding and hard graystone sill.

HITCHING

In the story, a car radio whines 1989: Van Halen,
last June's "Black and Blue." Thin tin treble pop
benign as the masticating sound of leather pants urging
in some back seat. Hijinks. You remember the crystals

on black silk cord—right?—the tight perms: mine to come,
Amber on her fourth, an asymmetrical cut. Lemon juice
to the roots. Ombré, before lean-to poverty hit the runway.
Hoops pierced into high cartilage because we weren't afraid

at twelve to get into a stranger's Chevette. Amber's father hadn't
yet taken a shotgun up the narrow stairs
                                        but the truth is there
was no music in that car. Only a scalpy smell, and bodies. Two men
drove ahead, silent, us in the hatch. I tell it as if there were grace-

ful streetlamps craning toward us, as if nostalgia drips like a willow
from my mouth. As if you, Reader, and I, have no reason to regret.
I won't describe the four-inch berm. The reflector tape flaring along
Orrs Bridge. Scottie waiting two miles down the road, breaking

a sheet into tabs. We were so young, clapping frogs across macadam
before blacktop could be laid. In fact I've never told this story—or have
told only a story, not what we swore that night, before descending
the creek-damp trellis. That we were ready to die, if it meant leaving

here, a life stretched and soft like our parents, counting days, dollars
till the next flood. The small abacus ahead. When the car pulled over
we rushed to the pockmarked door. Take us anywhere, we said
pushing forward on the seat, hard, until all we were was open road.

DEBT

The gray wave expects to clear our railings
by the end of today. Its rhythm is patience.
Cradled on land, then inhaled into walls,
water's in business with a subtle moon. They
have a plan but won't tell. You watch
the sea-foam simmer from the middle story
of a burning building. Its flames blow east
the way everyone predicted. It was a matter
of time, there was that night you fell asleep with
candles burning near the drapes, the day you left
a thicket of lint to choke the dryer. The fire forgave you
then, but you owed him.
       Just as you owe the earwig
who, for the third day now, waits in your phone's receiver,
pincers sharpening on the stone of their own mercy.
You dial someone to insist the worst
must be over. Can you hear him
tapping? There's a message
in his code: you're afraid
       of the wrong catastrophe.

FIRST PLOW AT RED MOUNTAIN PASS

11,018 feet below, the ravine does
its gaunt work, bringing matter
back to bone. The mountain sags
with the mass of endless storm
and you're first up, riding into
the cut. The plow's gears keen.
You shift, a question
more than a motion. Light
off the snow says morning.

Gravity's the only other
crew—gristled, wordless—
telling stories so natural
they seem untrue: tree roots
fused to the spine of a bull elk,
sprouting as antlers would,
had the head been left. How the skin
of a flat blue sky pulls taut, from
nowhere, matte, low, bowing
like a cosmic hammock
wet with stars. Then the split, the line
drawn thin by an unseen hand,
blade against pregnant cloud, shamelessly
delivering, spilling out a crowd
of white consonants, an argument
against the darkening afternoon.
We depend on things to fall.

You settle into the springs, no need
to rush the job. From up here
the big questions rattle like trinkets,
man-made things. Guardrails
would only crack or rust. In the dry
collarbone of a mountain, sentences end

with a still body. You've come first
after those reclaimed by the dirt, gray limbs
piled upon themselves like sloppy tinder,
and never wondered why
or how, or when. You work
until the work is done.

The woman in your bed
has no trouble sleeping. It's the slope
of the roof, she says, close
like a child's blanket
draped across two chairs.
For a few weeks each summer, quaking
aspen leaves turn in
on themselves against the cold
nights. Their wisdom is instinct. But out
on the pass it's the long season, one wall
of snow resisting the edge, fighting the fall as you
push; the other, a slant plane, mountainside, inclined
to wait, to rest a moment before
its shift begins.

Finger-drifts like smoke
from a coal stove call you
to the tunnel ahead, to the windless
sleeping place, if you can make it
there before the slide, someone
will remember how full
the sky looks from up here
always, how ready,
how still.

HERR'S RIDGE, 1983: A REENACTMENT

I think the knuckles in the wall will break
through tonight. The hollows hang there,

indentations his closed hand left once, and again,
shadows of instinct. People now don't speak

this language of apology, of small desperate joints
asking the sheetrock to stop closing in on a man.

We hear the narrow cabinet open. We are high
up the walnut tree, above the well rebuilt

after summer hail. The point of the old pine lies
on its side by the shed, and everywhere earth

mocks the carrot wood of repair.
In the house, heavy plates thrum on a table—

someone wants to know they can survive a hard fall.
Soon the tourists will return in new boots, to listen

for the ground's distorted heart. Their metal
detectors warp and whine into the fields' uncivil

core. They live for war. But won't trace the rabbit's
rapid pulse, bottom of the litter, drowning in nest.

Hushed by the squirming weight of the rest.
Even now, muscles thrusting, its papery flesh starts

to stew back into rich July soil—damp new face
we'll never see, still hairless, still blind.

The day after we say we don't know
each other or ourselves I drive our daughter
to the museum, to *White Rose with Larkspur
No. 2.* O'Keeffe haunts the canvas, a desert
shaped by wind. Her fingers twist along a wood
brush, as an arthritic pinyon
drills into or against layers of red stone and we
don't speak. Our daughter's brow resists this argument
for the hidden spectrum in white—we've taught her
cat from bird, engine from wheel. But here the petals open
to disclose their secret green, their yellow
blue pink gray. She is learning roots can be
branches can be shadows or hands
twining a woman's hair
depending on the light.

ANGELUS

Dalí's interpretation of a funeral scene was wholly rejected,
until an X-ray revealed Millet had first painted a child's coffin,
then covered it over with a basket.

Little mud shadow, hidden root,
only some of us know you were
here, ever a motion at all, a wave
before an arm, a seed just splitting
for the sprout. You lay coiled,
a comma, a question, the soft
green berry of a potato that won't
come true. I was a yellow stamen, then
a wheelbarrow full of empty sacks instead
of the ground you needed. You died
of thirst beneath the mass
of a basket. The painter understood
how to obscure and why
a prayer would be offered
to the brown earth and not to the ringing
of a brown sky. Dangers were everywhere:
a spire on the hill, pitchfork
digging for throb or pulse, we
were never safe. We were never
we, until Salvador, the man who bent time—
himself a closed eye, like you just
a part, a body's outline and no more—
saw the surface wrinkle with ants
coming forward to feed. You were their
small picnic, buried under a layer of reeds
by hands folded in hope, or by the dark
clutch of a fresh-tilled hunger.

SILVERTON

It doesn't matter who answers
the phone, it's the same forecast:
snow following snow,

road closed followed by Jessie
returning to John, wrist healed
and you can hardly tell anything

went wrong, until she waves hello.
Or is it goodbye. You know, this much
cold, this high, batters the eye

until all it sees is warmth. The girls
lining up crayons before dinner.
Coals orange as a daffodil's trumpet.

So easy to forget tomorrow's ash.
In a ghost town, bowls of thin soup
steam on every edge. Nothing

can hurt us. The pioneers. We forget why
we came—but look at that mountain.
Was anything ever so new?

WHAT WE SHOULD REALLY BE AFRAID OF

I

Not snow.
Not a single flake
and not all of them at once.
Not their nest, their melting
puzzle, their instinct to insulate
against heat.

Not the storm, even hard, not when wind
discovers rain let its cool mouth linger
on the spine of a high mountain.
Not the mountain.
Not the smooth mud that reassures its slope:
it's not your fault.

Not the thin white trees, leaning into weather
                        (they know what's coming):
                        portents, gray steam created
                        and dissolved like
                        an apology dripping down
                        a bathroom mirror.
                        Not the writer's hand
                        wiped on a leg.

Not spring, not another, not its vining
pleated limbs swollen with the ink of
a decomposing violet. Not the wasp
who shutters the hive of its compound eyes just
to live there, again, in that bloomy velvet—
reckless, forgiving, drunk with altitude.

Not the wasp's slender waist.

II

Water in the stream below buzzes
with struggle—a woman's hair
tangled in an anchor.
The thousand grasping hands of its rust
remind us: Pray that it holds.

There are things to fear.
You know it.
The water knows, too, the mountain,
the snow, even before it falls.
Boats, floating for a time,
wait for the sound of their narrow ribs
to crack. A fat speckled spider sharpens
in the shoe of someone you need.
Bacon grease naps in secret
cells.

III

A woman's thumbs fumble a button.
Her organs shimmy at the wrong
time, she tells herself it's
music. Someone else pulls a brush
through her daughter's hair.
She decides she won't hear
the steps in the hall, the key
turning in the lock.

He does it because he loves us.
You do it because you have to.
You do it because he told you.
We do it because we're told to.

In an attic, a man steps on something soft
and tells himself the whole floor was covered
with dead birds, so how could he not?
But there was only one bird, lying just
where the man stepped. He knows.
Through his shoe,
he felt the long bones of the wing
give.

II

FABLE

What if this year the scrawny splinters of winter refuse
spring's reckless flesh: its shameless, podgy vining
around stark limb, its honeysuckle undressing raw
to the fruit—profligate, easy with perfume, collagen
accreting in stalks like the slow-boiled gel of a bone
broth. The cold seems tired but has some good fight yet.
Let's not wake the hunter, let him doze awhile in his bough-
scented blind, dreaming of jumpy fawn-eyed stars. His rifle's
small crack, diver in a shallow splashless pool, can wait.
Reader, every year we get this moment wrong. Do we
know each other, our own bodies, our annual flex and bloom?
When you come to me, finally, overgrown, distended
with broad green leaves, will I remember where to lay
my hands, how to look away as longing, as lure?

WAYS TO DESCRIBE A DEATH INSIDE YOUR OWN LIVING BODY

If wavy glass feels old to you then sit down. I'm speaking
from inside the lead curve, where black minerals burn

to a shine like pissed-off soot suns. I was sure it was
a boy. I thought I knew the sound of darkness,

the slow leather collapse of a bat's wing
folding into itself, the swollen fucking of a cloud

of them wrestling for space on the cave's drapery—
let's call it what it is because that's how death begins, by tricking

your body into an arch, as if life will just tie a string to your spine
and hang there, a patient pendulum bob, waiting for you to finish.

No, inside the glass we see death clearly. First you feel limbs
(which, people remind you, you only ever imagined), then vague

flinting in the damp then the suck of wet bread separating
from its crust, then the white gloves around you flip inside

out and move on with the bright day
                                                    then you are far away

the deep cave you visited once, hollow, the planet's stone

core as it tries to carve out one secret place and fails.

You wait for a soft mouse above to spill out

of its hole, for the bats under your ribs

to flap toward some smaller pulse,

for the sun to give in, as it does,

so that the last headlamp can

finally click off and head

back into the night

everybody knows.

MOTHER OF 2 STABBED TO DEATH IN SILVERTON

—*DENVER POST*, JUNE 7TH, 2014

The woman was overheard in the town hall saying she was afraid
to do it, once and for all, that he would, like he's said, and he did.

That night the neighbors down Mineral Street heard the usual.
Words then cracks like biting into an apple and they felt bad

about it but what could they do. One woman cleaned a mirror
over and over. Her husband switched on the television, turned it up.

Who could they call at this hour? In the days that followed they would shake
their heads and give dazed interviews. A tragedy, yes. They knew

his father. It ran in the family, disgraceful. Suddenly they heard
nothing at all. The boys were home and everyone should have been

sleeping. They folded down their sheets. It could go a few ways.
Tomorrow she'd be out with the boys at the park, a little blue

peeking through her creamy makeup, but the sun would find
its way. They brushed their teeth and turned out the lights. It was late.

The footsteps came so slow up the porch they thought it couldn't be
anything desperate. He was covered in blood, and silence

hung over him like a new moon. It's dark but you know something
is there. It was an accident, he said, I never meant it. They stood there still

as newsprint.

LOCAL MUSIC

for Marie, in Silverton

You're four now, old enough.
You receive your first rifle,
pink, and a low target
on the dense foam bear. I worry
from so far. The forecast doesn't
bother with the Western Slope
and every day a coyote waits
patiently for the click
of the school gate, trots along-
side as you trip home. He's
sniffing the air for something
beyond sound, the tang of decay
dragged off Kendall Mountain.
From a distance, your mother
laughs, clearing smoke away
with a hand stout as a mallet.

What will you learn out there,
what will you hear, later unable to
unhear it? Even as this pen scratches
the page there's the furious cuff
of antlers against apple bark,
the old soundtrack of a country
one never really leaves: wind
rushing Martin's farm, a barn's baggy
Dutch doors tapping, bull calves inside
not yet sold. I still hear their dark
bleating song. The world, first, is local
music, then we are taught bellows
from harp, from shovel hitting ground.

Your rhythm won't be field but
mountain, percussing under crusted
snow. Already you know the notes
of collapse: wind slab, point release,
cornice fall. Under your jacket,
an avalanche beacon ticks
like a human heart. Soon the pass
will close until March—but your mother
says there's time. So I send you a book,
photographs of stained glass windows
pulsing in wild technicolor. Red robes
of monks unknown dissolve into iron
like cherry lollipops. Men conspire,
absolve over animals, altars, the pale
penitent heads of those unmonumented.
In exploded view, each pane froths,
tiny bubbles trapped in glass. You
and I rile them, laugh on the phone:
come up to the surface, if you dare!
—but they lodge there, patient,
the way melting snow never
really goes anywhere, just returns
first to the ground, then back into
air, part mineral, part memory.

GETTYSBURG

The peacock's spurs are caught again
in the diamond chickenwire of his low
slanted pen. Nobody bothers anymore
to hammer the sagging barn.

Summer visitors regard the old farm from cars
without chrome, up on the hastily paved path—
if they look at all. There's so much
else to see, burnished things, and battlefields

all look the same. But it's here, this land,
where the war's easy sepia finds an end
and a form: like us, the shallow rust-red soil
blows off for York, for Philadelphia, the coast,

and pasture erodes to bone. A black walnut's roots
pierce the buried limbs of our grandfathers' fallen
spruce grove. The caterpillar inches along, lost
in its sad accordion hymn.

ADVICE FOR THE NEW MOTHER

Mornings, hands will pull at the new folds of your body until you produce something worthy of a mouth. So take bread, and butter the bread and hold it the way you would a face, back when you wondered what a face might hold. Carry the bread on a plate as it gazes up at you, at your face, wondering where it's headed, to whose mouth. The bread is no longer an object, but a series of calculations: coordinates of the dense spherical eye a tired surgeon moves from one body to another. The hollow socket gapes like a wet hatchling. All the while the eye, the bread, the child gazes up at you, insistent on its new home, optic nerve dangling like the sooty roots of a hopeless plucked beet, like the tentacles of soft russet coral swaying, inert in waves so deep they're only sound. Beneath your shirt, the coral's fleshy tubes stand there breezing, waiting for warmth and motion, for the vibration that compels them to seize and to release their sour-clot milk. This is breakfast. This is what you wanted.

CROWN CINQUAIN FOR THE TATTOOED MAN I REFUSED

—rather,
for the tattoos
I've never forgotten:
thick, bruised Hebrew, scripture-stung skin
unread,

      index
finger drawn down
his body's hard thirst. Swells
of ink humming, storm-stirred, between
our ribs.

         Reckless
restraint.
What would have sung in us,
what prayer worthy of the temple
we were?

     A flag
waves lazily
across the street. I swear
I could hold this wind in my teeth
all day.

HE WAITED FOR DAYS

When he was five or maybe six, their car
broke down in Pennsylvania. They rolled
to rest beside a silo. Served her right
for dreaming somewhere else, somewhere new—
there's rotting corn spilled out in every road.
Leaving was decisive—fathers did it.
But this was still the forties, his mother
told him to hide—no porch lights, no one called out.
He watched his mother's dark familiar shape
grow dim, then unfamiliar, not a body, more
a wind that uproots fields and just moves on.
She pitched the keys skyward to buy time—
by morning, when they found him, she'd be lost.
He was alone then, five or six, or less.

AS I NEAR FORTY I THINK OF YOU THEN

And if your face were younger I'd buy you
the house you've always wanted. Big red door,
wreath heavy enough for a swallow's nest.
I'd make good, in your language. Clear view
of the coast and of the road that runs along it.
Shortbread every morning, boats in the distance
so you can depend on something coming back
better than it left. As it is, you are almost
seventy, wincing without moving your lips, though
you'll deny it. You feel like a poseur now, a stranger
you say, at the beach. Once it was all you knew.
Bonfires and tan stomachs. Anyone could have
loved you. I'm sorry for what's next. You, stranded
at a gas station in Ohio. Infant surgery and
the cast that followed. Years my father spent
quoting the Bible as you swept and stewed, saved,
let out hems. While we kicked and bickered
your thirties away. If I could go back to the dark
farming soil, I'd rip out the hyacinths and plant you
a lifetime of hydrangeas. You'd find yourself
there, between chestnut trees. Sand and all.

WHEN HORSES TURN DOWN THE ROAD

*Until we crossed the Md. line our men behaved as well as troops could, but
here it will be hard to restrain them, for they have an idea that they are to
indulge in unlicensed plunder.*
—MAJ. GEN. WILLIAM DORSEY PENDER, C.S.A., TO HIS WIFE, JUNE 1863

First, both rings into the hollow clock.
The clock, then, behind a canister of flour
on the pantry shelf. At this hour shadows
will soften edges. Candlesticks
under a floorboard, use the old book

to pound it back flat, just like he
showed you, before wiping his neck
with a slow hand, before waving
from the yard. Work the third stone
out of the hearth's floor, papers folded

and folded again, bring the children
to your skirts. Turn their faces away
from what comes, from what will
be done, stand as these soldiers' own
mothers would stand. The small

white shoes on the mantel can
stay—some things won't be taken
no matter how many boots cross
the gate, no matter how wide
you open your own stone door.

LETTER TO MY FOUNDLING: #235, BOY

The two halves of this city pull at the stitches.
River unwound, a wooden spool turning to loosen
its coarse gray thread.

It was me who

When you were born I

I was the mother joining scraps for a sleeve.

Your mottled chest rose and fell as I unpinned
my hands from your gown. The breathing—still
wet, still sudden—I could see it aspire:
oilskin stretched across new whalebone.

You were my sea-tossed lamp.

I was the boat, the
kerosene, spilt into a dark current
where cloth would only pull you below
as someone you once knew, a body
around your body, made for
the shifting sea.

MEMENTO MORI: BELL JAR WITH SUSPENDED CHILD

I

A crow circles the dome. One endless wing
anchored, axis, in fresh-bloated ground.

The other, feather-tip, skims glass sky—that coil
of perpetuity, surfer's thumb along barrel wave.

Here, my daughter is no more than simulated
landscape, spring-loaded copse woven of her

plucked hair. Love become thatch. Trembling palm
tree rooted into diorama of waft, wander. Quaint

surgery, the modelmaker's hand.
                                    I want to say no,
to the bent note, the queasy calliope reeling from this

jar's base. As if turned earth sings, as if a mother might
trade grief for the whine of a candy flute. Go on, dark

crow, drift—you, too, born of my ribs. Your span
whirls like the dancer's foot in a music box. Always,

the wrong ones leave us.   Bird, inevitable bird, where
should you land

your arrowhead   beak,
                                    if not in me?

II

The quality is: days pass. Fork-colored fan blades
warp stuck air into a hymn. All warbles toward rot.

You salt what you can hold—lamb chop, cartilage.
The brute snout that once sensed a hunter's vague fear.

Over time—it could be centuries—toes web, widen
against sucking mud. Please stay dry. But the body,

sick brilliant machine, creeps, breeding the yeast
of strange fever, effusing into garden—the traitor.

Explosions of promiscuity: coral peonies, lady slipper,
gape-mouth jewelweed.

Where do I put the rage?

On the child's bed, one doll has been stitched inside
another.   Women are meant to carry things to safety.

But here, scissors grind out a requiem: tooth-gnash of a girl
lost to brassy, desperate death. Only, the lonesome

death. Who needs a hand small as hers?—its ease,
its locomotive warmth? Remember, the spirit

hath fled.

            Every spot we touch on the living fossilizes
toward object.
                    This is a stung, hollow song,

and the lungs that expel it—flabby, vestigial, like the heart
of a prey whose low branch has just been lifted.

III

For a woman's bile to rise high enough, it takes years—
years to cure it, to a keen, to age the wild broken hawk

blood into wine, the musk to metal, aloneness a mineral
swelling her milk-marble eyes. Stiffening the chute of each

hair, smoothed, pinned back like a moth's leg under glass.
Somewhere, a hand tugs the knots from inside her

ship's bottle, hoisting toothpick masts to sail
for nowhere.
    Shouldn't we end on a shelf?

Shouldn't the orb-weaver eat yesterday's web?
Watch her climb the net of her own hunger

to snip filament, filament, anchor, swallowing
the whole fine, diaphanous delta, nautilus whorl,

line after line funneled into the pocket of a gland.
Just another mother gathering blankets from a bed.

The spider knows tonight she'll knit again, reflex
unspooling the drab meal into muggy honeycomb,

measuring out the tessellations of a dragonfly's sight,
and again tomorrow, taking in until the world's ready

to take back, her form sliding along the same remade silk,
pendant on a chain.
    The faith of instinct. Instinct of faith.

IV

Bell ringing in an empty room

  Heavy curtain, heavy wind

Bell ringing in an empty room

  Under the stairs, mold in a vase

Bell ringing in an empty room

  Sky overcast, basin filmed with lather

Trembling bell, empty room

  Thank you for doing what I cannot do

Empty bell, trembling room

  Metronome, woodpeck, hammerfall

Empty bell, trembling, trembling

  room, ringing womb, rinsing

room of the body, the bell

  hollow, holy, tolling up, out like

horse hooves pealing through

  streets no one travels, but us

V

If he can't fill me how will I be
whole? With the gape of me
bulbous, raw, the sap of a torn peach

trickling, how? How with every shiv
blunted, too dull to stab this pulsing
tenderness? Outside, bodies pass

in and out of each other. Barges
bump against a lock. In the dark
a man and a woman lie

on the quay, joining, unjoining,
gathering what they can, as if a small fire
has suddenly surged.

If he could, he would drink this river,
find the child at the bottom. Strangle the swan,
and wrap our hard love in its wings.

VI

It's difficult for the bat to understand the other limb
of this argument, so bent on survival. Listen to him
tell us: fur-necked hissing half-bear, half-cobra.
Like water, the man says, they get in everywhere.
But tonight you make no calls. You are vision, mercy.

Sounds of the bat's drowning: iron dowel squealing
inside steel pipe, metal unfinished, unthreaded, crude.
Listen to the way the pillow's down settles
under the weight of your body. How it streams
into the bat's nose, flat as a crushed heart. Listen

to the nothing. To your blood doing its stupid work.
A ruined animal will drag itself miles, only to become
a desiccated hutch, burrow of maggots, coyote trough.
The opossum, pouch-heavy, will shelter in any cow's husk
and if rain hardens to sleet, will den in the rind of another

opossum.

Somewhere, there is a long hall, filled with jars of all sizes.

I will save you this end.

VII

It's a hundred years later—three hundred, more
—and I'm stuck in the sad lattice of a foreign cemetery.
I'm lost. Stray dogs snort into the pink dusk, joining up
like magnets. Flags rooted in the yard start to blur beyond
stripe, day's red wilts to russet.
                              I've looked for you
everywhere, the mausoleum's stacked slabs, in cracks
spanning grimed glass like fragile rivers. In each globe
of glue dripped like dew on tomb flowers, clotting,
punctuating the arch sheen of petals that were never
petals at all. I'm listening here, for your paw-sized voice.
I ache for it. Me.   Me. Because how else
should I tell you I can't remember anymore
the scent of your new skin, still crusted with salt
of my body? My ancient body, its residue of a life
under water—hair so like mucousy kelp, strung
with cysts plump as beans, furious as a gland's small mill.
How will you know to close the gate, to go? Leave me
here. The dogs grow hungry, as they should.
They know the way, they'll bring me back to you.

III

WESTERN SLOPE

The women who come here partly give up
being women. No last names, no locks.
A spike, instead, concealed in every hairbrush.
A man's a bear, a cub embeds his claw
in the hollow door. You wear it on a string.

Your own first snow melts gradually, old firn
riding the continental divide back to a distant
ocean. We swam there once, that water, alien blue
algae pulsing like a showgirl in the wings, it was
when you shot the worn dog that I knew you

had gone for good. Even cakes struggle to rise
at 10,000 ft. Hard angles to the atmosphere, you
say. A newborn fits a thick palm. Blood stretches
too, gasping, for its sliver of air. You won't come
down, everything now's an open mouth to the wide sky and the sky unspooling cloudless
                    and cloudless and cloudless.

            (But—before I go—wasn't it us for a while? Weren't we the neon
            kicking in the light? Tell me you remember the waves
                            bathing our necks, our small ears?)

WHALE FALL

During sleep, a whale shuts down
only half her brain, and these days
I know how she feels. The term
is conscious breathing, if she forgets
everything's done for. Down into the depths
like defunct electronics, massive and gray
as a tanker full of jammed mimeographs.
Better to keep one mild eye open, stoned
as a dusk-fed cow, than to risk slow-sinking
into the pulp of the sea floor. How do we ignore
the stealth of the anglerfish? The soft force
of lungs crushed past equilibrium?

Anyone who finds the sea placid
hasn't been paying attention. A dying
whale descends, enormously,
toward special humiliation: to be jungle
gym for twitchy neon fish. Fondled
by scurvy eels, then gnawed into plankton.
Nothing left of the effortless menace,
the casual hunger of baleen swishing krill—
all of it, gone. Instead of the sea opening
like a purse, pouty mouths peck,
gumming at our lead pleats, only to spit
and suck and spit again. The nerve. All they want
is our algae. This, for decades. Until our long
bones are finally exposed, raw, the pale frame
of a once ambitious ship, now aimless
as sugarcane wrapped by shrimp. Tonight, we pull
our sail from a dryer, flail. Where would we go
if we went? We can't recall what sleep
ever meant. *Whale fall*, scientists call it.

For a mammal the size of a metro bus
route, the whale does lack some imagination.
All these years, not a single fin reaching out
for beach plums. (Do you know what's still said
about L's mother, who left her kids in a mustard-
colored playpen and drove toward sunset?)
On the other hand, the whale's skeleton, once
picked clean, still pinches into two tiny
leg bones, just below the tail. Think of it:
what they might have become, had they
developed a taste for our dry air—or
had they not turned back. Their bulky city,
vast hospitals specializing in joint repair.
Instead, woozy bags of organs, little more.
Even with those hearts big as rental cars.

But the bit of fur, the milk remind us
to Windex the lens before we aim
and shoot. If we look close enough we see
ourselves ticking along to magnetic north:
this way for food, this for sex,
how to enter a current, and to escape,
the way shade quivers when orcas circle
a calf. We remember how to begin
again, day after day, letting others moor
or latch as the ticking clock requires. For us, life
drags on for two hundred years. Half-breathing,
half-awake, floating or swimming—we're not
sure which: but push out/drag in, through
the blowhole flexed as a starved nostril,
we're at the surface for a flash, foaming
plum, plum or was that from our mouth,
beak, pineal gland, appendix, the flukes

we can't shake? We can't say which, or where
we are, or when we split into legs—didn't we
live here once?—but which direction
to summer, unthinking lung? Lung, it's been so long
since we've dragged against a new shore,
carved a sandbar into a question mark.
Muscled along the freshwater beaver's tail,
well out of our own water. Just listen to all
the claws out there, clicking along
unfamiliar strands. Breathing, any way
they can, as if real sleep might arrive
with the next wave.

IF IMAGINATION AND MEMORY MET UNEXPECTEDLY, ONE LAST TIME

it would be this moment, the dark slow mess
of one body unpiling toward another in sleep, the longing of two
waves reeling in queasy parallel. Mostly it's like you

never rested here, this body, your head never heavy
as sorrow, as troubled bone, never turned in my palms
like an artifact, gently undisguised. I shouldn't remember

you as the trim boat you never were, this place
as a storm. There are errands now. Children.
On the second floor of the world, a tepid bath fills.

Some people will bear any anchor through
the endless flaying tide. Our ocean unraveled quickly
into salt—but listen, for a second, as we used to

         —do you hear it holding us
    there, scraping against the old
        undertow? Minerals under motion,
           rock inside swell—no,

shell, just shell, dry-littering the wrack line.

MORNING TEA

You could say we tried it all. After the small body was
swaddled, boxed, after we closed the lid on our gray

snail, on its shell too like cartilage, after translucence
clouded into opaque chalk, after the long black car

returned to a far garage, after the words exchanged, punctuated
by the hardest consonants we could muster, stored away

then dropped. Anvil music. Before the morning tea blubbered
in its pot. You could say we tried everything.

     Ours is a porcelain world, thin, bonded with some unknown
     compound—and us, silent, at a table where all we drink are grains

     of loose sediment: a mixture, a mineral
     someone insists will cure all it touches.

MINE FIRE AT CENTRALIA

At one point voices clattered like black stove doors.
The mine chewed and hawked. Beneath this viscid town
a swarm of locusts sensualized. No one needed the future

to shine—it glinted, a hunk of anthracite jutting
like the villain's hard jaw. Things were easy
to classify. You and I drove in on the only road

left, years after eminent domain, after the place had been
hollowed above ground, too. Wire fences unrolled to keep us
from questioning what might have been: your temple

vein slept for once. Instead of the car, our world
idled, a film of sulfur steam frothing the ether
between us. We lay in the remaining grass, two lone

row homes of a ghost town, buttressed by spalling brick.
Stale as a cut planet's crust. We knew something about that fire,
why they'd let it burn so close to the vein, how it spreads.

Under your shirt my hand dislodged a sore sullen ember,
dank, the sweet smoldering peat that would consume us
before I'd ever agree to pack up and go.

STOPPING OVER THE ARNO

For all we know they only paused
on that bridge. It was evening or might
as well have been, toucan-orange low
along the water, smeared to the keystone.
It wasn't a real place—they tell themselves
that now. But where else would she murmur
what she never will again, breath thick as the rain-
swollen wheel of a wood cart, discernible words
blurred by his thumb, what was once her
mouth, *sfumato*.

        If we could find our old
lexicon, the book would offer alternatives
for *love*. Something wetter, green paint
drying without a sign. One pear hanging, left
on the tree, beaded with relief and resignation.
She wouldn't let him touch her as he had,
forcelessly. Here, arched over a river swallowing
its impulse toward current, balanced on a curve
shallow as a sloth's long claw, she couldn't
imagine not remembering his head, turning
as it had heavy against her fluted ribs.

Were we ever there? She wouldn't recall
his hands securing her waist, the railing,
its dim rot. Even now she can't hear the flags whip.
The breaking sky. The salt in a man's voice
shouting *Accidenti!* as wind from no direction
billows a woman's cotton dress, lifts it
into the clouds of another time.

CITY LIFE

My four-year-old starts to rename everything
in terms of rats. At first the playground
behind our apartment: *Rat Park.* We visit
a rose garden, then suddenly it's *Alive Rat Park*
vs. *Dead Rat Park.* She's young enough
to fear the living more than the dead, the way
they hug the garage walls, run marble-eyed when
we return at dusk. I hear her laugh at the blue bike
some new tenant has fence-locked by the nest.

She's learning to live a city life, asking
if I've heard that, and that, tipping an ear
to the alley, cupping it with her hand
small as a raccoon's paw. For her, death
is the longest nap imaginable,
maybe four hours. But we always wake
at the end. I think of telling her, but don't,
how I used to be afraid of rats—a transplant,
more accustomed to field mice who'd come
in through the Dutch door dividing

cornfields, forest and grass airstrip beyond,
how my first year here I stopped rush hour
to wrap a hit pigeon in a blanket, insisted
on some natural dignity for the squirrel
fallen from a tall Brahmin tree, brains frozen
to the blacktop. How I tugged, then
wrenched. But never for the rats. For months
I stepped around the fat wolf-colored one

skull-knocked by a parking Jeep outside
my office, as it grew flat and flatter, gas
and liquid and old poison leaking into familiar

ground, until just tufts of rind and hair remained,
and only for those who remembered.
How I kept my distance, day after day until
I came to love him, just in time.

FLIGHT THEORY

Gorlice, 1908

Wstawaj, don't | You turn off the lights this time and
speak, he will | lie still, a body shifting from its country,
wake, and come | climb gaunt gray waves into a sky built
for you. My hand | deep within the fat matter of memory. Stirring
over your mouth is | his tongue, he slips into your wet speech,
our goodbye. | dismantles you quietly, rot threading plaster.

His black | Organs are everywhere: on the workbench outside
feathers stir, no | animals left unskinned. Empty socket stuffed with
wind, oil upon | a dirty rag, only you know about the snake
oil, his long beak | pushing through high grass. He'll slough until the world
shines. Take this, | offers an indifferent body. (Who can be choosy?)
I have saved | This, your life—what is a stepfather for? For emptying

it all slowly in | a ribcage, the warm meat of your parts lost as
a shoe, zrób co | his hands undo—your mother will say wings, whispering, but in
mówię, lodge it | truth—you lose yourself under a loud human neck,
in the gathers | its gulping skin stretched over bones, over low vowels
at your waist and | you pray no one hears, not even you. These voices, glottal,
never exhale. | they travel with you, to Kraków, Hamburg, Cuxhaven, Nowy Jork,

Run, road to station | to the factory where you cart bobbins in a skirt, again and again
to the dim nodding ship. | arriving full, departing empty: sound rimming the lip of a bell.
Szybko. You will know no | Windows too narrow to let the light in. Dark swells
one. If you hear me | in your quiet inner room, like a mushroom sponging into root.
calling you, moja | New world daughter threaded with horsehair worms, their
córka, close the | small farm sprouting even under your fingernail. Once you had a

door to us. Run | past: the tremoring kerosene lamps, the hard stone roads still
until dark birds | come for you. But now shadows buckle into static, a man sent to
hang, shoreless, | the distant tinfoil moon, doing nothing but walking, without gravity.
aimless, land | As if ours were a small world, well lit, the sounds you hear only footsteps
disappearing like salt | across the dust of a slackening galaxy; you, a mass of ice slow-spiraling.
in a stirred glass. | Your young son flaps from the screen, *what is it like, Mamusia, to float*
away?

WHAT FALLS BEHIND

The first sign was a fluted bead, ruby, glass, mixed in
the dustpan with shards of translucent cat claw, magnolia
petals, ash from a fireplace long ago stoppered and sealed.

I'd like to say we pressed at mantel seams, shuffled
closets to see what needed repair, but—though we knew
this wasn't debris from our living—we lowered the lights

and slept. As if alone. The new moon sometimes lets dark be
what it means to be, and you ask who it is I've seen,
man, or woman, an age, what room. I tell you it's a ripple

of the mirror, hardly a form at all, more a sense of rushing—
then, absence. I tell you someone's been here, is here now.
We hear her knock from behind the wall, she's up

late again, dancing the Charleston with hands loose
as tassels, gleeful, grinding the soles of her shoes into the beam
that supports us, supports everything we think we know.

NO RESPONSE

By which I mean I used to hear
the hair on your face stir before
it curled through a single layer of
skin. By which I mean over-
coat now, green wool too long

to wear to any farm. By which I
mean prissy, urban, disconnected
from the pliers used to dock sheep.
From the rough brushing with bent wire.
By which you can take the girl out

of the country by which I mean bleating
on a loop. Meaning some songs play
beyond sound. Gregorian green singing grass
growing, roots pushing from below till
everything's got to be shorn within

an inch of its life, meaning the world
meaning sweat upon blue-wet organs.
Back to our bodies. Meaning crescendo.
Meaning instinct. In other words the truck
is in the drive. Meaning we've been here

before, fetching the block. The quiet
that follows. We have touched the edge
meaning the blade, meaning that line
between injury and surgery, meaning us, by which I
mean it will take us both, two pairs of bleary

cloud-crowded eyes squinting through
the barn's dusty slats, to read the score,
the new tattoo black-branded
into a ewe's raw ruddy-cool ear: Love,
walk with me, past the gate, into the only honest place.

RECURRING DREAM

Cottages so close, the low thatch
knits to a canopy beneath which

you, humid and inert, drag your legs
as if to run, round white bulbs

sagging like clotheslines and this could be
a party, come to think of it, bodies

in red taffeta you can hear swish
and jostle, so don't need to see

the slow scrape of a tango heel
along weathered wood—or his face

recognizing yours, after all
these years, moving wordlessly

upstairs, two ghosts ready to finish
what was never, in daylight, begun.

CROWN CINQUAIN FOR A LOST CHILD, EIGHT YEARS LATER

Now I
hardly wince
when clapping moths. My skin's
grown used to absorbing its own
hunger.

　　Crushed hay,
iridescent
smear of ground-cherry husk:
I knew you once, your wings still gummed
with dew.

　　　　A heart-
beat's rhythm—hard
to unhear. Subway trains
rattle across thick bolts of track.
Vacuums

　　　　yawn, their
endless doppler
swallowing afternoon.
In dreams, ultrasounds fill my room,
flood it

　with blue,
your alien
dance a cipher, a plea.

How could such otherworldly grace
live, here?

AT THE PARK ONE DAY, MY SIX-YEAR-OLD ASKS ME
IF MERMAIDS ARE REAL

Can you blame me for saying yes? This week
a middle-aged man walked through the glass
doors of her elementary school and proceeded
to the boys' bathroom. Outside, a girl gripped
the chains of the hard-spun tire swing in a move
the kids call *flying grandma*. Barrettes slid down
her hair, each long ribbon tied off into a tiny
morningstar. Boys in a dirtcloud dug at the planet.

A secretary heard the man's obscenities grow
louder, walked toward the stalls. Have you ever
tried to balance on a dome of black elastic web?
I don't know how they do it, untroubled engines
in cotton-candy tutus and superhero T-shirts, even
mermaid tails. The world is an ocean, that much
is true, and after, the custodian brought a bucket
of salt water to clean away what the man had done.

She asks me if mermaids are real, squinting her
whole face as if she's swallowed the sun, and I'm
so relieved I laugh *of course*, aren't we overjoyed
that all he did this time was shit, all over the floor,
lonely, but alone. *If you close your eyes*, I say,
you can imagine it, right? For now, we'll hide
in the abstract. The park sprinklers spin, shoot
a fizzy mist, opal droplets glinting like fish scales.
Kids running, swimming, holding their breath.

AS IF THE WORLD MIGHT HOLD ANOTHER

A few days after I turn forty-two
I spend an afternoon sifting through
drawers of infant clothes—unworn
hangered, smoothed, the stained or torn
sloughed off into aimless piles. Why
not make room for the unfilled? Only I
ever knew about the tiny capelet, the cloche,
the quilted red leather boots. We approach
middle age as undiscovered country when
really it's the same old alley, the bowling pin
that wobbles like a drunk but won't go down.
All stories end in flood or drought. Tartown,
1993. Ditching trigonometry, we'd measure
back roads instead, listen to treadle threshers
squeal across the pond like bedsprings
coming to. School wasn't as much things
you learned as how much you could resist
and we were bright, so bright. It doesn't exist
now, Tartown, its groves of hollow blackgum
drowned under a reservoir, the tar kiln's crumbled
chalk dissolved, limestone lapped back to shell.
Where the hot sap's gone off to, who can tell?
The first of us to get pregnant said nothing,
floated on her back like a pinecone, opening
and closing, contracting in the damp. To drop
seeds seemed pointless in a landscape throbbing
with so much ninebark, moss, maidenhair fern.
Along the water's surface, we took turns
sweeping each other through the shaggy thatch
of needles, like mothers swirling the bath.
Don't misunderstand: there was no romance.
We carried hard regrets—still do. By chance
we were there the day they brought cranes
to scrape the basin. Instead of membrane,

stripped wood planks were spread, caulked
with their own warm pitch. We never talk
about those visits, at the weddings, on calls
that come less and less. The nursery walls
hang, still painted neutral blue—robin's egg,
as if the world might hold another spring. I'd beg
to be a nest again, one more time, but how
to fasten this mangle of fresh grass to this dry bough?

LOCAL HISTORY

The earth says have a place, be what that place
Requires; hear the sound the birds imply
And see as deep as ridges go behind
Each other.
—WILLIAM STAFFORD

No one thought about a mountain beyond
the yard, thought to stare past the lusterless
wire pen steaming with yellowjackets, no
one said *disappointment* or that wheelbarrows
rust once glazed. We waited for the truck
to deliver the mail or load the calves, fathers
to arrive at night or not to arrive, the rising
moon indifferent. Fireflies zagged lambent
down in the tavern's gravel lot, past the S-curve,
where generational drunks loitered heat-bellied:
arguing seed or battle strategies (so much depends
upon history), which route to the lake, hesitant to go
home when the dark's so rich, damp. Where I am
today, island of gawky seagrass and lavender stalks,
a mystifying brine hangs in the air: What could grow
here? This salt must scorch, or does it preserve?
If I could go back, ask the knot of guts gathered
down the road, would they hear me calling from
behind the ridge's tailbone? Not knowing them,
you'll question, despise them for their stained-
pine rifle cabinets, knobby as spines, their thick
thumbnails used to screw and to plane, to halve
the licorice rind of dog ticks. Carl and Ed, Jesse, Ab.
Even half-cocked they knew the silo was leaning.
Could tell if the stale, bruised sky would wring out
its hurt or hold it, predict the hour a kettle of hawks
would spiral, ready to blow, would burst into boil.

RIVER BONE

The cat slips through   the closing   door
as if I have   a secret only   she   knows.
She's come to inquire, say   the angles
of her   face,   a lizard's   trapezoid
softened by   fur (providence
of   geography) and by tonight's blue
light   hazing   off an unwashed mirror.

Once,   in a canyon of the San Juans, past the line
where dirt   divides into eras, allegories, I knelt
for what lay   white, coiled, a parched fossil
shell: ammonite   ram's horn, nautilus vacated or
harvested, uncrusted   a relic. Oh anklebone
of water, vertebra of   the Colorado, still
gnashing, still red!   The etymology of desert
waves rushed in   to articulate, a current
unwinding itself   pulse against membrane.

The cat's mink is a handful
of impossible ash.   She knows
the story,   the bleached skull I couldn't
identify the next   morning   —muskrat? rock
squirrel?—so tight to my straining   it clung
like a scorched whisper, a dam   restless, unsprung,
until the succulents   muscled into root, swallowing
night's thin vapor, an ancient sun turning flesh again
to bone.

HONEY

Of the sheep's four stomachs,
which would we jar, which stir
into tea? *Abomasum, omasum,*
reticulum, rumen. Amen. Cud
does loop the gullet like prayer.
And lettuce-hem *reticulum* shares
its name with the honeycomb's
net. But for a throat flayed raw
who among us would slice
the distended balloon, harvest
its porridge the color of bloat,
spoon it on a child's tongue?
Tell me how honey's different.
Even bees, crocus-drunk, split
their nectar, guttering most,
flume-like, into the loose purse
of a second stomach, sweet syrup
reservoir. Once back at the hive,
each bee regurgitates its swill into
the rapture of a waiting mouth. Gut
to gut, so nectar passes, in chains,
the fury of 20,000 wings boiling off
all water. And what do we produce?
What sap? Bees' profound necking
falls beyond our French kiss, closer
to the queer plunger of live birth.
Yet, in the dim thrill of evening
we advance. Why does a body turn
inside out like a sleeve at the soft
shock of lips unsealing, letting us in
and out like a canal's lock? To those
I have kissed, on granite stairs and

idling trains, under a roof cut out
to frame the sky: What passed
between us? How did it harden?
Whom does it nourish now?

DISASTER AT GOLD KING MINE

If you were to write a letter in your own hand, say
I'm coming to look for you, all the words we let slip then
lost for good would flat scuttle, back out from the stull timber
we propped ourselves. *I promise you.* Fractures, by design.

Even silverfish await their turn to play Big-West stars,
metal-drenched but shallow as pans of sifted glitter. It's
been awfully long since we raised a hammer to anything
hard. We came for gold—all's left now is the sallow bile

of a billowing river. Animas. Out here anything real
ends up jaundiced. Don't let me tell you, this is no story
about fish bloated with cadmium, about foil lures grown pale.
I'm not saying a thing about that strange glow rising like heat

from scabs of scaly rock.

Say it. Let the ancient water come.

Let mine runoff swallow this mountain whole, its small coast. We
won't miss the riverbank. Let mica flint-twitch as it, as it all, wakes
to memories of swimming how we did too, once, the world itself
steeped in new luster.

THE BIG THINKERS

Listen to me. When he opens the door covered in black you think you know that half grime–half growl color, same as the runny coal slurry that coated our skin while we swam in the Conodoguinet, before any dam held things back, what we assumed was just ancient mud jumping up from a seam in the pipeline like enthusiastic licorice, you think you recognize in his fingernails that same dismal pudding we took into our mouths just to spout it back into the creek, rotting waves dotted with shredded inner tube. Those rubber bits were everywhere—remember?—after that boy drowned. The man who jumped in to save him drowned, too, first in fact, but not before his back flashed at the surface stained with the same dense shadows you've seen haunting your husband's work clothes, or think you see, thick as hide, well after you've sung the kids to sleep. I'll say it plain. We're not from there. Out west things are big under a big sky with clouds you have to imagine hard it's that blue. Blue the way people on coasts insist water should be because it once was, somewhere we've never been. The color of nineteenth-century dreams, elemental and distinct, as if each object in the world had just emerged dripping from a vat of pure pigment. Unambiguous. Red earth, green trees, white stars, and under it all: gold. Gold the color of a man in a new suit, walking around town with no one to answer to. Listen. I'm telling you we don't know that man. Out there they're big thinkers, necks like dragons ready to fly until the mountain peaks leap higher with hungry gold flames. Big, big, shipping whole yards of equipment over the northern ice to that island in Alaska, an ark stocked with pairs of ridiculous fantasies, when the snow melts for a few weeks in summer that island's just waiting like a glass candy dish, waiting for them to come stick their hands in, so much gold it's a cancer, eating away at the red soil until the ground itself could sink to the bottom at any moment, down into the hollowed-out space, they'd better get there and quick, once it's down only divers can get it and have it and flash it and spend it. Big. Fat bankrolls swelling in an imaginary pocket is them while our people just do, slowly, in the dark low mines of Bethlehem, Centralia, wiping coughs away with a thick sleeve, knocking at the walls of loose dirt with an axe the size of a cocktail spear, chipping away at the dark rock till the vein shines, but only slightly and if you have your headlamp, you see our scale isn't big, we're the thin pink lung of a winded canary, watery yellow or less even, the color of barely breathing feathers so light they could carry the bird and all those big thoughts too to some warm place, somewhere bright like a Sunday walk, all of us spewed out on a single gust from the ventilator. Back here knees sprout roots in the sludge, we're setting up for a long dark day, not discovering just uncovering and dragging generations of shovels across the wet streaks somebody says should be right about here.

RD 8 BOX 16A (RURAL ROUTE)

I miss the ugly things: sallow
flypaper crusting in porch sun,
bootlines across shit-caked denim.
The dog's staph-eaten paw
soaking in a Cool Whip bowl.

No lemonade sweating on a sill:
I want the penny loafer testing
a rumble strip of rusty nails,
Betadine's kidney-smear stain.
I want the sour ferment of rotting

hay and the funk of whatever it is
that's died between the walls. I'm
ready now, made to scrape grease
from the brick hearth, to sweep
attic bats, to drown the raccoon.

Outside, a kind of rainy season:
yew bushes shedding their coal-
colored seeds as if to hide all
evidence. When you're young
what you don't know can kill you

can flush your lips with berrywine.
Tasha's up the road, laying heavy
from the busdriver. The boy I won't
name aims a rifle at his cousin. There
they stand, smiling, breathing hard.

Let me keep them here, with us,
relax the finger's pulley, coil this film,
stack it in a glossy gray tin. Praise the dirt

breeding in a cut, how easy methane-drunk
air parts for buckshot's meteor shower.

What ache is this, that mimics a wireworm's
slim boreholes? I wash a dish, feel nothing
but phantom cornstalk, kernels swelling
as my hand smothers silk grubs with oil.
So much gold, everywhere, gold—how

did I not see it? Gas lowered, the skillet still
spits. The pond, untroubled, swallows any
splash. This raccoon's not thrashing, it's just
a dance, his eyes' yellow glare nothing more
than a reflection, of some old rising sun.

BEAR FIGHT IN ROCKAWAY

Up till now it's been a story about ivy
pulling down arches. Pipe cleaners shifting to dust
in the attic sun. We've stopped worrying so much
about worrying. Lights on a dimmer.

Then suddenly, bears: at the mailbox,
at the door. We hear them first, their strange
digital mooing, their pendulous throats.
They shuttle dark sounds back into our range

past the wood gates we've built or let
stand, through storm screens coated in rubber.
Their blunt heft shimmers under swipes of claw, fur unspooling
like a reluctant accordion. And we are glad

to see them, old friends, the torque of their patient combat,
even here, even as a child blows soap bubbles through
a grooved ring, even as bathwater cools around her chest.
The way the bears' bodies linger before they strike, mouths

open, slack—we remember something of that, from before
all the fences, the stairs and the cars, from a similar injury or kiss.

NOTES

"Week Six of the Fire" borrows its "I have faith" refrain from Aimee Nezhukumatathil's "Upon Hearing the News You Buried Our Dog."

In "Herr's Ridge, 1983: A Reenactment," the image of the falling dish comes from the unpublished poem "Two Bowls," by my friend, the poet Rachel Beck.

"First Plow at Red Mountain Pass" is based on stories told by Rusty Melcher.

"Fine Arts" makes reference to Georgia O'Keeffe's *White Rose with Larkspur No. 2*, part of the permanent collection at Boston's Museum of Fine Arts.

"Angelus" refers to Jean-François Millet's painting *L'Angélus*, part of the collections at the Musée d'Orsay.

"What We Should Really Be Afraid Of" alludes to the print *pray the anchor stays heavy, my child* from UK artist Hidden Eloise. The poem's final stanza recalls a story told by Mark Levine.

"Local Music" makes diffuse reference to Robert Frost's "For Once, Then, Something."

"Gettysburg" describes Brown's Ranch, known during the Civil War as the Emanuel Pitzer Farm, which was recently sold to become a beef cattle operation.

The cinquain form in "Crown Cinquain for the Tattooed Man I Refused" and "Crown Cinquain for a Lost Child, Eight Years Later" is an invention of Adelaide Crapsey.

The epigraph in "When Horses Come Down the Road" comes from a letter in *Civil War Letters: From Home, Camp, and Battlefield*, edited by Bob Blaisdell.

"Letter to My Foundling: #235, Boy" was inspired in part by swatches of fabric on display at London's Foundling Hospital. From the hospital's opening in 1741, mothers were asked to "affix on each child some particular writing, or other distinguishing mark or token, so that the children may be known thereafter if necessary."

Section I of "Memento Mori" describes a domed memento mori hair "landscape" recorded in John Whitenight's *Under Glass: A Victorian Obsession.* Section III's "filament, filament" alludes to Walt Whitman's "A Noiseless Patient Spider." Section IV echoes a line from Robert Hass's "Sketching Techniques" lesson, a video offered through the University of Iowa's International Writing Program.

"If Imagination and Memory Met, Unexpectedly, One Last Time" draws inspiration from Carl Phillips's poem "The Jetty."

"Flight Theory" is an imagined reconstruction of my great-grandmother's late adolescence. She was about sixteen when her mother woke her one night in Poland and, without warning, ushered her off, alone, to America.

"River Bone" alludes to the "handful of intangible ash" in Elizabeth Bishop's "The Armadillo."

The epigraph in "Local History" comes from William Stafford's poem "In Response to a Question."

"Bear Fight in Rockaway" responds directly to J. Domzalski's YouTube video "Bear Fight Rockaway NJ August 14 2014."

Please note that in some cases names and identifying information have been changed to protect others' privacy.

ACKNOWLEDGMENTS

Sincere gratitude to the editors and staff of the following journals, in which poems from this collection first appeared (occasionally in earlier versions):

American Poetry Review: "Ways to Describe a Death Inside Your Own Living Body"

Baltimore Review: "If Imagination and Memory Met Unexpectedly, One Last Time"

Borderlands: Texas Poetry Review: "River Bone"

Boston Review: "Bear Fight in Rockaway"

Calyx Journal: "As If the World Might Hold Another"

concīs: "Silverton"

FIELD: "When Horses Turn Down the Road"

Florida Review: "Hitching" and "City Life"

Greensboro Review: "Angelus"

Gulf Stream: "As I Near Forty I Think of You Then"

Journal of Compressed Creative Arts: "Advice for the New Mother"

Kenyon Review Online: "Memento Mori: Bell Jar with Suspended Child"

Los Angeles Review: "Flight Theory"

Measure: "He Waited for Days"

Mid-American Review: "Letter to My Niece, in Silverton, Colorado"

minnesota review: "Herr's Ridge, 1983: A Reenactment"

Mississippi Review: "Fable"

Missouri Review (Poem of the Week): "What We Should Really Be Afraid Of"

NANO Fiction: "Self-Portrait as Cenotaph" (as "Gettysburg")

Nimrod: "The Big Thinkers"

North American Review: "Whale Fall"

Penn Review: "Fine Arts"

Pleiades: "Week Six of the Fire" and "Crown Cinquain for a Lost Child, Eight Years Later"

Poet Lore: "Stopping Over the Arno"

Quarterly West: "Local History" and "RD 8 Box 16A (Rural Route)"

Shenandoah: "Gettysburg"

Sou'wester: "No Response"

South Dakota Review: "Mine Fire at Centralia"

Southwest Review: "Miscarriage"
Subtropics: "As for the Glossy Green Tractor You Were" and "Recurring Dream"
Sugar House Review: "Local Music"
Southeast Review: "The Clearing"
Tahoma Literary Review: "Mother of 2 Stabbed to Death in Silverton"
Tinderbox Poetry Journal: "Debt" and "Letter to My Foundling: #235, Boy"
Valparaiso Poetry Review: "First Plow at Red Mountain Pass"
Waxwing: "At the Park One Day, My Six-Year-Old Asks Me If Mermaids
    Are Real"
ZYZZYVA: "After the Police Have Been Called"

Thank you to Bill Henderson for including "The Clearing" in the *Pushcart Prize XLIII* anthology, to Dana Gioia and David Lehman for including "Miscarriage" in *Best American Poetry 2018*, and to Tracy K. Smith for selecting "Western Slope" for *Best New Poets 2015*. Thanks to Lindsay Hunter for choosing "Letter to My Niece, in Silverton, Colorado" as winner of *Mid-American Review*'s 2014 Fineline Competition. Gratitude to the folks at *Florida Review* for honoring "Hitching" and "City Life" with the 2017 Editors' Award and to Cheryl Boyce-Taylor for picking "Flight Theory" as winner of the 2015 Orlando Prize from the A Room of Her Own Foundation. Thank you to Jean Sprackland and John McAuliffe for selecting "What Falls Behind" as one of the finalist-awardees of the 2015 Troubadour International Poetry Prize, and to Anne-Marie Fyfe for the poem's subsequent publication.

This book would not exist without the wisdom and patience of my former teachers—especially C.D. Wright and Marvin Bell, whose own work and whose personal generosity continue to inform and to inspire me. Somehow you believed in me, and took the time to say so, despite my poems that hadn't yet received all you'd given. To you both, my unending gratitude, here and in the next world. Thank you also to Forrest Gander, Gale Nelson, Robert Coover, Michael S. Harper, and Charles Mee; and to Mark Levine, James Galvin, Marilynne Robinson, Robert Hass, and Dean Young—for your intellect, your example, your humor and humanity, your practical guidance, and your willingness to believe writing might be taught. To Judith Church, F. Jane Scott, Naomi Duprat, and Selby Doughty, across years and miles: thank you.

Thank you to my friends, who have supported and inspired these poems and their author: Chris Castellani, Eve Bridburg, and everyone at GrubStreet; Kari Croop, Arian Hassani, Eliza Hammel, Kendra Harpster, and Natasha Lake, for cheering me on; Joe Pan, Tim Lake, Tim Krcmarik, Reed Smith, Rachel Beck, Anna Ross, Jennifer Elmore, and Debb Bennett, for your friendship, your careful readings, and your ongoing influence. Thank you to John James for your guidance through this process, one you know better than anyone! Thank you to my former colleagues from Boston University, whom I miss, and to my current colleagues from Boston College, whom I cherish; to my students, a constant source of energy and purpose; and to Howard dePass, Jr., my Poetry-on-Demand partner in rhyme. Wild fields, ripe orchards, and whales of gratitude to Kim Garcia, Sue Roberts, and Skye Shirley, respectively, without whom there would be no book, no poems, no writing life.

Sincere thanks to Maggie Smith, Eduardo Corral, and Marcus Wicker for carving out time to read this book and for gracing it with the support of your voices.

To Henri Cole: My heart is so full thanks to you. For selecting *The Clearing* from the many worthy manuscripts submitted this year, for your generous correspondence since, and even more for your own exquisite poems, please accept my deepest gratitude.

A huge thank you to everyone at Milkweed, that impossible dream team of realizers, anchors, tireless harvesters: Daniel Slager, Lee Oglesby, Mary Austin Speaker, Yanna Demkiewicz, and Shannon Blackmer. Thank you all for every minute you dedicated to this book, and for the kickass catalogue you maintain year after year. Special thanks to this year's Milkweed Fellow, the fabulous Julian Randall, for approaching this manuscript with both depth of feeling and expert attention.

Max Ritvo's poetry has featured in my reading and teaching for several years. Together, "Poem to My Litter" and "The Senses" serve as a kind of refrain for how one might approach life, with permeability and care for truth. The honor of this sudden association with Max's work and legacy is difficult to put into words. Thank you to Max's family and friends, especially to Riva Ariella Ritvo-Slifka, and to the Alan B. Slifka Foundation, for this deeply meaningful gift.

Finally, all love and appreciation to my family of Adairs, Carusos, and Greens. To my parents, the source of every blessing. To Lisa, Marie, and Bonnie, my wild-flowers. To Georgie, my world beyond this world.

To Max, my love, forever, wing to wing, oar to oar.

Max Green

Allison Adair's poems have appeared in *American Poetry Review*, *Arts & Letters*, *Best American Poetry*, *Best New Poets*, *Kenyon Review Online*, *North American Review*, and *ZYZZYVA*, among other journals. Recipient of the Pushcart Prize, the Florida Review Editors' Award, the Orlando Prize, and first place in *Mid-American Review*'s Fineline Competition, she holds an MFA from the Iowa Writers' Workshop. Originally from central Pennsylvania, Allison Adair lives in Boston.

The third award of the

MAX RITVO POETRY PRIZE

is presented to

ALLISON ADAIR

by

MILKWEED EDITIONS

and

THE ALAN B. SLIFKA FOUNDATION

Designed to honor the legacy of one of the most original
poets to debut in recent years—and to reward outstanding
poets for years to come—the Max Ritvo Poetry Prize
awards $10,000 and publication by Milkweed Editions to
the author of a debut collection of poems. The 2019 Max
Ritvo Poetry Prize was judged by Henri Cole.

Milkweed Editions thanks the Alan B. Slifka Foundation
and its president, Riva Ariella Ritvo-Slifka, for supporting
the Max Ritvo Poetry Prize.

Founded as a nonprofit organization in 1980, Milkweed Editions is an independent publisher. Our mission is to identify, nurture and publish transformative literature, and build an engaged community around it.

milkweed.org

Interior design by Mary Austin Speaker
Typeset in Adobe Caslon Pro

Adobe Caslon Pro was created by Carol Twombly
for Adobe Systems in 1990. Her design was inspired by
the family of typefaces cut by the celebrated engraver
William Caslon I, whose family foundry served
England with clean, elegant type from the early
Enlightenment through the turn of the
twentieth century.